Mail Carriers
at Work

by Karen Latchana Kenney
illustrated by Brian Caleb Dumm

Content Consultant:
Judith Stepan-Norris, PhD
Professor of Sociology, University of California, Irvine

magic wagon

Meet Your Community Workers!

visit us at www.abdopublishing.com

Published by Magic Wagon, a division of the ABDO Group, 8000 West 78th Street, Edina, Minnesota 55439. Copyright © 2010 by Abdo Consulting Group, Inc. International copyrights reserved in all countries. All rights reserved. No part of this book may be reproduced in any form without written permission from the publisher.

Looking Glass Library™ is a trademark and logo of Magic Wagon.

Printed in the United States.

Manufactured with paper containing at least 10% post-consumer waste

Text by Karen Latchana Kenney
Illustrations by Brian Caleb Dumm
Edited by Patricia Stockland
Interior layout and design by Emily Love
Cover design by Emily Love

Library of Congress Cataloging-in-Publication Data

Kenney, Karen Latchana.
  Mail carriers at work / by Karen L. Kenney ; illustrated by Brian Caleb Dumm ; content consultant: Judith Stepan-Norris.
    p. cm. — (Meet your community workers)
  Includes index.
  ISBN 978-1-60270-650-7
  1. Letter carriers—Juvenile literature. I. Dumm, Brian Caleb. II. Title.
  HE6241.K46 2010
  383'.145—dc22

8/10   2009002398

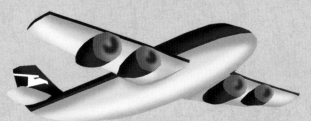

Table of Contents

Being a Mail Carrier

Do you have a letter to mail? A mail carrier will pick up your mail and deliver it. Mail carriers deliver letters, magazines, store advertisements, and small boxes. They deliver mail six days a week.

4

A mail carrier gets signatures for some mail and boxes. If a person is not home to sign for a delivery, a mail carrier will leave a note. The note tells the person where to pick up the mail. Sometimes, a mail carrier has to collect money for mail costs.

Helping Others

People in cities, small towns, and the country get mail. Mail carriers work on certain streets or parts of the country. This is their route. Sometimes mail carriers answer questions. They might deliver forms or sell stamps.

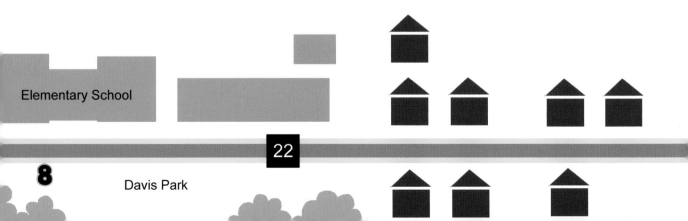

Elementary School

Davis Park

Church

Hickory St.

Cherry Way

Parking Garage

Gas

Hospital

Grocery

Lincoln St.

Library

Franklin Hwy.

Mail carriers meet many people in a community. Some check on older or sick people on their route. They also watch the streets in a neighborhood. If there are problems, a mail carrier will call the police.

At Work

For the first part of a day, mail carriers work inside a post office. They sort the mail into a tray. The mail is put into bags or a truck. Then the mail carrier works outside for the rest of the day. The mail goes to mailboxes in houses and apartments, on the road, and in offices. The mail carrier also collects new mail.

On their route, mail carriers work alone. At the post office, mail carriers work with other postal workers. They wear blue and gray uniforms. In the summer, they wear shorts. They change to warm clothes in the winter. Mail carriers also wear a patch. It shows an eagle's head.

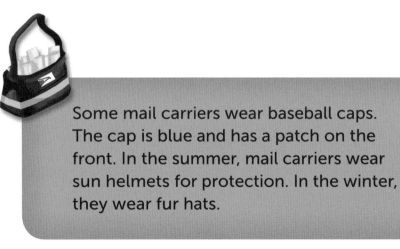

Some mail carriers wear baseball caps. The cap is blue and has a patch on the front. In the summer, mail carriers wear sun helmets for protection. In the winter, they wear fur hats.

Problems on the Job

A mail carrier's day starts as early as 4:00 AM. A mail carrier might walk long distances outside. Working outside can be hard. Sometimes it rains or snows. This makes sidewalks and roads wet or icy. An important part of a mail carrier's job is to keep the mail safe.

17

Tools Mail Carriers Need

Mail is sorted by address into a tray. Some mail carriers put rubber bands around each bundle of mail. A mail carrier puts mail into a bag called a satchel. It holds 35 pounds (16 kg) of mail. A mail carrier also puts mail in a satchel cart. Then, he or she rolls it down a sidewalk.

A mail satchel is blue and has one strap. It has a shiny stripe on its side. The stripe helps people see the mail carrier.

A mail carrier walks or drives to deliver the mail. In most cities, mail carriers drive a postal truck. The truck is white and has a blue picture of an eagle on its side. Mail carriers in rural areas often drive their own cars to deliver the mail.

Mail carriers drive postal trucks from the passenger's side. This allows drivers to reach mailboxes along the side of the truck while still driving in the correct direction!

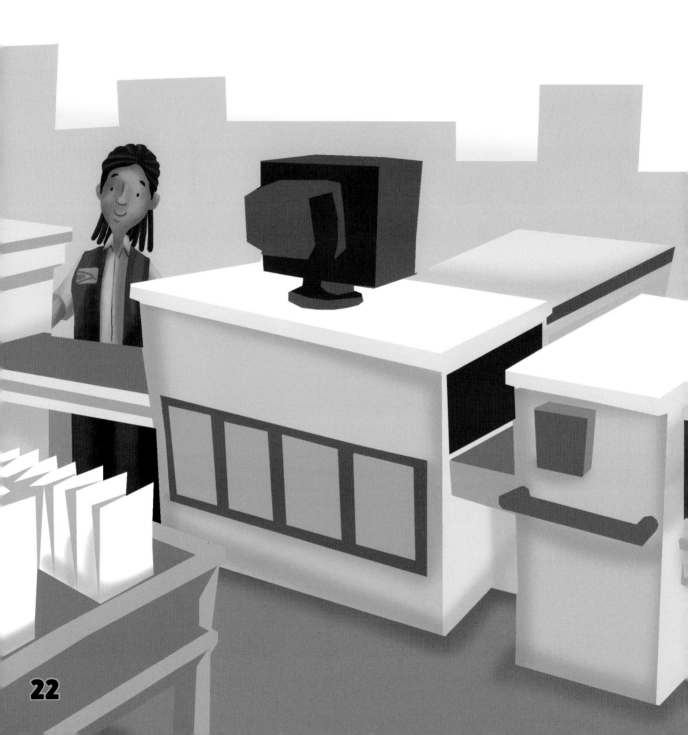

Technology at Work

Some work is done before a mail carrier gets to the post office. A machine reads addresses and separates the mail by route. This makes work easier for mail carriers. They spend less time sorting mail. It gives mail carriers more time to deliver the mail.

Special Skills and Training

Mail carriers need to like working with people. They must have good speaking and reading skills. They also need to remember things. A mail carrier has to be healthy and like to work outside.

Mail carriers have to be at least 18 years old. A person who wants to become a mail carrier must take two tests. One is a written test. The other is a physical test. Mail carriers need to lift 70 pounds (32 kg). After a person passes the tests, he or she is trained at work.

In the Community

Is there a letter in your mailbox? Mail carriers deliver mail to many places. They help people stay in touch with each other. They also help businesses do their work. Mail carriers are important workers in every community.

A Day as a Mail Carrier

Early Morning

Start work at 4:00 AM at the post office.
Sort the mail by address.
Put a rubber band around each bundle of mail.

Late Morning

Put mail bundles in the postal truck.
Start driving on the mail route.
Deliver mail to an office building.
Get a signature for a box.

Afternoon

Put mail in a mail satchel.
Walk in a neighborhood.
Deliver mail and get new mail from homes.
Check in on an older person on the route.

Late Afternoon

Drive back to the post office.
Turn in new mail and signature for the box.
Stop work for the day at 2:00 PM.

Glossary

advertisement—a printed notice from a store that shows goods or lists a sale.

bundle—a group of things tied together.

deliver—to bring something to a place.

post office—the place where people buy stamps and send mail. It is also the office where mail is sorted and goes out for delivery.

postal workers—the people who work in a post office.

route—a line of places that are visited by a mail carrier.

rural—relating to the country or farmland.

satchel—a bag that is carried on a person's shoulder.

signature—a person's name written on something.

Did You Know?

A dog named Dorsey delivered the mail in California in the 1880s. He walked between the towns of Calico and East Calico on his route.

The Pony Express helped deliver mail between 1860 and 1861. Men rode fast horses to deliver the mail. They would travel up to 100 miles (161 km) each day.

The U.S. Postal Service has more alternative-fuel vehicles than any other business in the nation.

On the Web

To learn more about mail carriers, visit ABDO Group online at **www.abdopublishing.com**. Web sites about mail carriers are featured on our Book Links page. These links are routinely monitored and updated to provide the most current information available.

Index

DATE DUE

GAYLORD

PRINTED IN U.S.A.